4-4-2 vs 4-3-3

An in-depth look at José Mourinho's 4-3-3 and how it compares to Sir Alex Ferguson's 4-4-2

by

Michele Tossani

Published by
WORLD CLASS COACHING

First published January, 2009 by
WORLD CLASS COACHING 15004 Buena Vista Drive, Leawood, KS 66224
(913) 402-0030

ISBN 9780979994876
Copyright © WORLD CLASS COACHING 2009

Author - Michele Tossani
Edited by Tom Mura

Published by
WORLD CLASS COACHING

Table of Contents

Page 4   -   Introduction

Page 5   -   José Mourinho's 4 - 3 - 3

Page 45   -   Sir Alex Ferguson's 4 - 4 - 2

Page 84   -   Mourinho's Key Chelsea Players

Page 87   -   Ferguson's Key Manchester Utd Players

Page 90   -   What We Can Learn From Mourinho and Ferguson

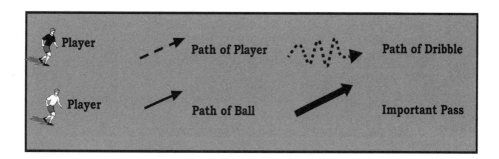

4-3-3, 4-4-2 and 4-3-1-2. Those are some of most utilized patterns by some of the most covered coaches in Europe.

And, between these coaches, you can find Josè Mourinho and Sir Alex Ferguson.

They are two of most prepared coaches in Europe.

In this book, I tried to analyze their system and their approach to the game.

In addition, we also have some suggestions in how to utilize those systems.

You will find some examples on how to utilize a 4-3-3 and a 4-3-1-2 against the most popular pattern in the world, the 4-4-2, and how you can utilize the 4-4-2 against the 4-3-3 and the 4-3-1-2.

So, you can find a way in how play a match as if you were Sir Alex Ferguson or Josè Mourinho.

Also, you will have a brief list of things to learn from those great coaches.

José Mourinho's
4 - 3 - 3

Chelsea FC

José Mourinho's 4-3-3 formation worked well during his first season with Chelsea FC.

Arjen Robben, Damien Duff and Joe Cole split time as offensive wings, while Didier Drogba played as a lone forward.

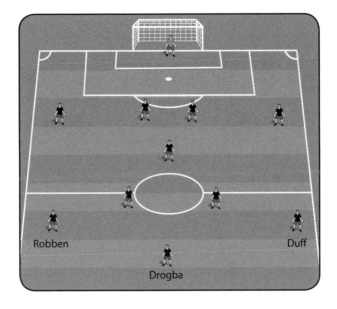

With Michael Ballack and Andriy Shevchenko in the mix, Mourinho quickly switched his patter from a 4-3-3 to a 4-3-1-2 system.

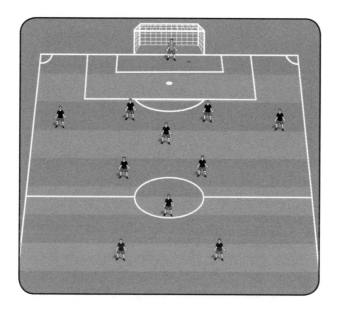

Differences Between the Two Systems

In general, there are some differences between the 4-3-3 and the 4-3-1-2 system.

The Advantages of the 4-3-1-2

- an attacking midfielder behind an offensive combo;
- two triangles of players, one in the middle and one up top;
- a great central defensive organization, with an holding midfielder and two interior midfielders ready to cover the defensive corps;
- the unpredictability created by the midfield combinations

The Disadvantages of the 4-3-1-2

- it's difficult to cover the flanks, with just one player on each side;
- geting the attacking midfielders to help cover on defense

The Advantages of the 4-3-3
- the unpredictability give by the slants of the wings;
- the chance to spread the field
- a great defensive compactness due to the wings' come back and play a 4-5-1 in the defensive phase. That pattern covers the whole field
- the chance to play a high pressure defense

The Disadvantages of the 4-3-3
- this pattern requires great physical condition
- if the wings don't come back, midfield is in trouble in the defensive phase
- high risk of counter-attacks

How the 433 is effective against the 442

The points in favor of a 4-3-3 against a traditional 4-4-2 patter are:
- a 4 men against 2 men on defense;

A superiority in the middle, where we have 3 men against just 2 midfielders;

And, on offense, the opportunity to keep the opponent's defense spread out, having three forwards which cover the whole offensive front. Having two spread wings force the opponents' fullbacks to stay deep and defend rather than make runs forward.

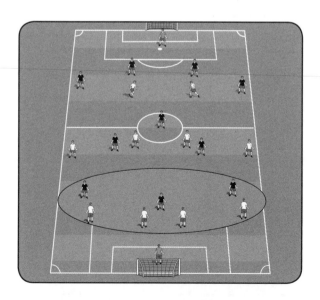

Schemes

We can start our attacking play with short passes from the back to take advantage of numerical superiority against the two forwards.

If the opponents press the central-halves, they can open the play by passing to the outside backs.

However, if the opponents pressure the fullback, we have a 2 v 1 situation in the middle to initiate the attack

If the opponents send a wing to help the two forwards pressure the ball, the defense still has a 4 v 3 advantage.

If the opponents send four men to play a very aggressive pressing action, the defenders can send a pass to the middle, where they can play a 3 v 2.

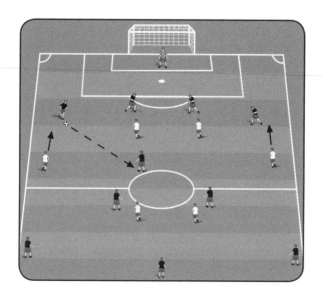

Another offensive weapon for the 4-3-3 against a 4-4-2 pattern is the play of the playmaker.

This player is very deep and he can play the ball relatively unpressured.

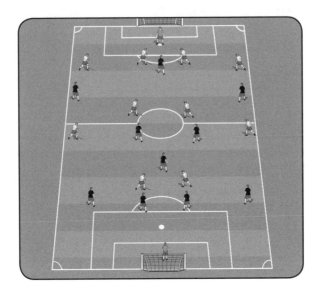

Some teams are set up to press this playmaker. They press him by dropping a forward back.

Occasionally a team will crown the middle by moving the midfielders inside. If the opponents play this way, they have to leave the wings open in order to cover the central midfielders.

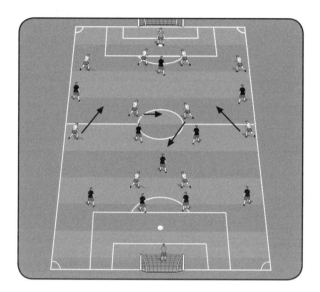

Both of those solutions play into the hands of a 4-3-3. In the first scenario, we have the opportunity to play moving towards one of the defenders. In fact, we can play on the side without the opponents' other forward.

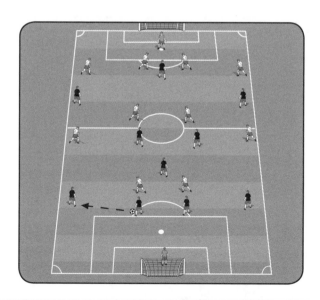

In the second scenario, we have the opportunity to play inside for one of the other central midfielders.

Otherwise, if the opponents send the full back to cover our defender, we will have space behind the opponents' left back to play with our wing.

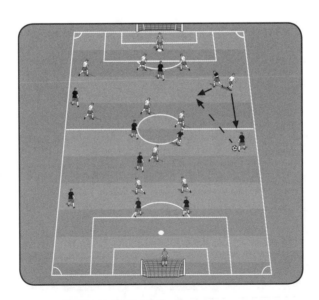

So, we can see that moving the "outside chain", formed by the triangle defensive back-interior midfielder-wing, we can play a 3 v 2 situation against the opponents' defensive back and outside midfielder.

If the ball goes to the central midfielder, we can utilize some of Mourinho's solutions against a 4-4-2.
- If the playmaker is covered by a midfielder, the 4-3-3 has 2 other midfielders free to play

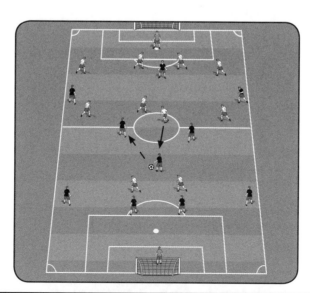

- If all the midfielders are covered by the opponents, we can send the ball outside;

With the ball in the attacking half, we utilize the wings to spread the opponents' defensive back four men line and the central midfielders as attackers.

Indeed, defenders will have to choice between:
- stay wide open to contain the wings

- or stay tights to cover the attacking midfielders

In both situations, the 4-3-3 has the advantages.
- With the defense wide open, there is a 3 v 2 situation in the middle of the defensive zone

That give us a clear numerical advantage in the middle of the defensive zone.

So, take a look at some examples of how to run the 4-3-3 against the 4-4-2 in the offensive zone.
- defense moves the ball to the wing.

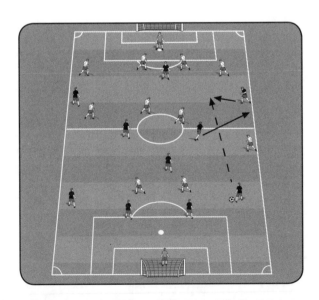

Wing can passes the ball to:
- interior midfielder overlapping;
- to the lone forward moving inside with a slant;
- to the other attacking midfielder inside;
- to the opposite wing moving inside with a slant.

Another classic movement is:
- ball from the fullback to the wing inside;
- pass back to the interior midfielder;
- pass towards to the fullback overlapping.

The key to his system is using the lone forward as a pivot/playmaker to move the opponents' defense and to open spaces for the upcoming players.

Here is a typical pattern involving the lone forward:
- ball to the lone forward;
- pass back to a midfielder;
- two options for the midfielder: pass on his side to the wing or switch to the opposite wing.

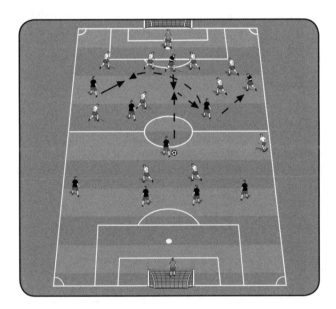

If, as often happens, a defender marks our lone forward, we can play a 3 v 3 in the attacking zone.

Changing the point of attack from one side to the other.

The opposite wing has to read well the situation on his side. So, if opponents' fullback play a short diagonal, our wing has to stay wide.

If the opponents play a long diagonal, the wing will play an inside slant on the weakside of the 4-4-2 defense: the zone between the fullback and the center-halve.

In the first seasons of Mourinho in Chelsea, the Portuguese coach played a 4-3-3 pattern.

His 4-3-3 isn't a classic 4-3-3. This isn't an ultra-offensive formation, a complex system with wings doing complex movements inside and central midfielder and defensive backs all ready to jump into the box.

In fact, Mourinho's approach to the 4-3-3 is more conservative. In the offensive phase, Mourinho's 4-3-3 is based on the wings' play.

Flankers played very spread, to open the opponents' defensive systems.

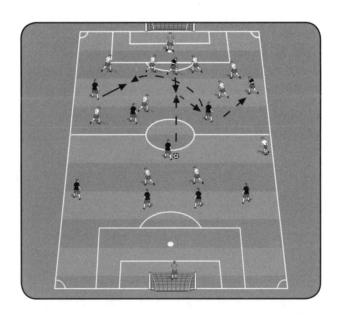

They were able to play inside with slants,

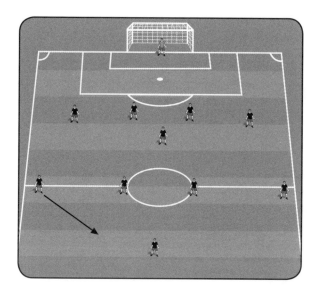

or go deep to play effective balls into the box.

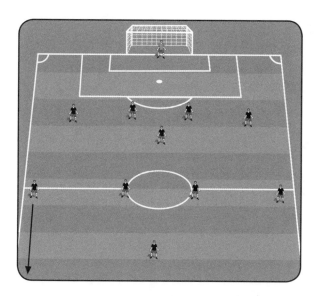

Near the box, In the Mourinho's 4-3-3 wings can go into the box directly;

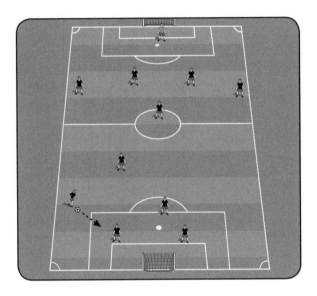

Or go outside for the cross.

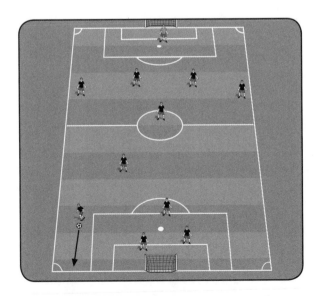

For example, with the ball on the right side, the central forward, right wing and one of the central midfielders are ready to go inside.

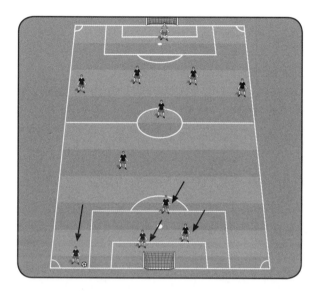

With the ball on the left side, the central forward, left wing and one central midfielder to go into the box.

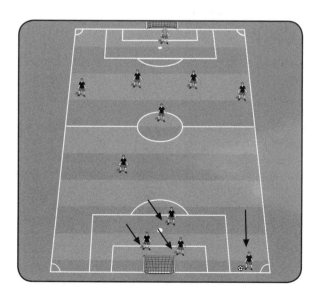

With Joe Cole, Mourinho had a winger who likes to go inside between the opponents' lines.

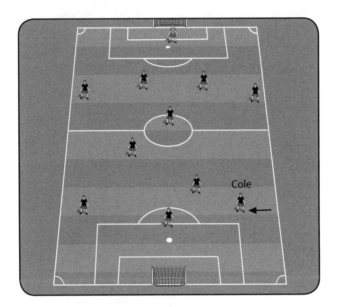

Mourinho was able to win despite not having many goal scorers, with the exception of Didier Drogba.

The key to his system, and his whole coaching approach, is to place the right man in the right place. No wings in the middle or holding midfielders on the flanks to cover, but every player in his best spot.

Mourinho's 4-3-3 relied on a central midfielder like Fank Lampard.

Lampard's Skills

Lampard is a classic midfielder, able to play both the offensive and defensive phases. On the offensive side of the ball, Lampard is able to go inside to score or to play good passes for the offensive trio.

Having an "inroad player" from behind is a good way to destabilize the opponents' defensive systems.

The 2007 FA Cup final was determined by a 1-2 punch by Lampard and Drogba.

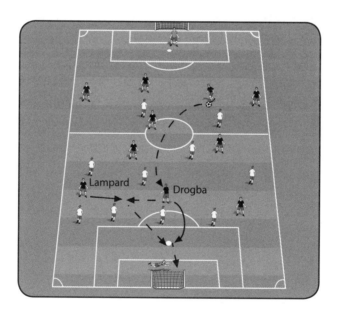

The defenders were trained to play a long ball for Didier Drogba when they were being pressed by the opponent.

The offensive key for Mourinho was (and maybe always will be) to send the ball to the forwards soon as possible. His teams are able to close the spaces, stretch the field behind the opponents' defense and play quick counterattacks.

First the team, then the individual. It was a solid and practical team. It was a team known for his high percentage of clashes won.

The holding midfielder duo of Geremi and Makelele built a wall in the middle.

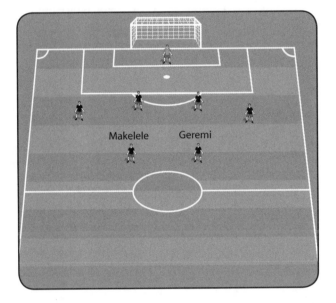

Makelele is a different type of playmaker: he's not a technical player such as Claudio Reyna was, but he's a pure holding midfielder. His first goal isn't to attack but is to break the opponents' attacks, delivering simple passes to the more offensive teammates.

Those passes to start a new offensive action could be:
- towards the outside;

- towards the inside;

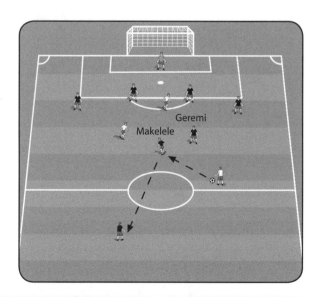

Mourinho's style at Chelsea was clear: when the team can attack, it attacks; when the team is pushed back by the opponents, it's ready to play quick counterattacks.

Those counterattacks are, at times, played starting the offensive action with 10 men below the line of scrimmage (line of the ball) so they start with a long ball to the lone forward.

If the lone forward can goes towards the goal, he plays alone, trying to score.

Here is a look to the Drogba score against Liverpool in the 2006/07 season:

If the lone forward can't goes directly to goal, he plays together with the midfielder from behind and with the wings to build a scoring chance:

Here is a look to the Drogba's score against Watford in the 2006/07 season:

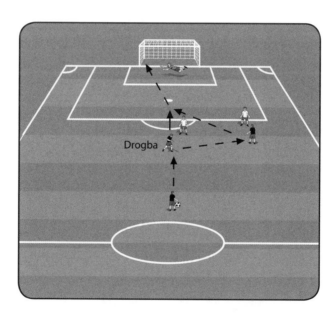

Mourinho's Chelsea wasn't a team that just played a long ball as some teams do.

One of the most common ways Mourinho's Chelsea would score was the shot from outside the box. In fact, many goals were scored with direct shots from 20-25 meters.

But the key of the Mourinho's system is the transition phase. Mourinho often left 5 players in defensive position when the team attacked.

In fact, when an offensive player lost the ball, everyone but the lone forward would come back quickly to build a 4-5-1 formation to protect the goal. So, he has 10 men employed in the defensive phase.

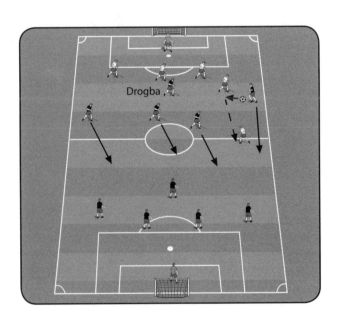

It means that he would stress quick counterattacks with long balls.

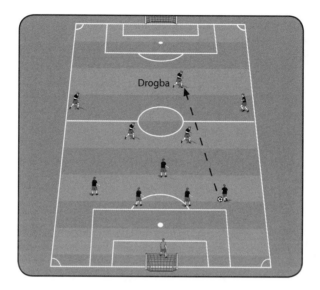

In the defensive phase, Mourinho didn't play high pressure in the other teams half of the field. He opted to begin pressuring at the top of the middle third or farther back, near the box if necessary.

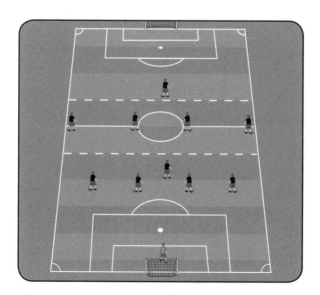

Even when pressing, it's more of a press done by 1 or 2 players near the ball more then a collective pressing tactic.

Defensive diagonals are used with one line of coverage.

Defenders rarely support the offensive phase. Their first goal is to defend. Mourinho likes big, tall defenders.

When the ball is on the outside and goes back, defensive line didn't push up very much, but maintained their position, with the holding midfielders as a wall in front of the defensive bunch.

When German Michael Ballack and of the Ukraine Andrey Shevchenko came to Chelsea, Mourinho switched his 4-3-3 formation to a 4-3-1-2 pattern.

Despite Shevchenko not playing much, it's important to take a look at the guildlines of Mourinho's 4-3-1-2.

The offensive policy and the playing traits are the same then with the 4-3-3 formation.

Attacking Traits
- very quick counterattacks
- great use of free kicks
- speed and quickness to move the ball from the defensive zone to the offensive zone (positive transition)
- mix of short and long passes;
- ability to attack the spaces between the lines
- intensity play
- when a player is in the box, the first goal is to shoot on goal

With the 4-3-1-2 against a 4-4-2, the first goal is to utilize the presence of an attacking midfielder between the opponent's lines. This is hard to cover by formations without a low midfielder.

This system has 2 playmakers: one in the own half and another in the opponents' half.

The roles and responsibilities of the low player are the same as the playmaker in the 4-3-3.

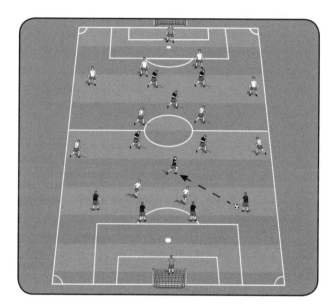

This gives the team a great central advantage then in the 4-3-3 pattern. In fact, we have 4 central midfielders against just 2 of the 4-4-2.

So, a good tactics is to send the ball quickly at one of the central midfielders.

The width can be utilized
- moving up the outside backs;

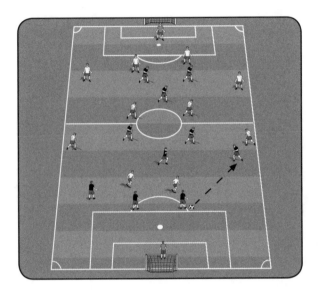

- moving towards the interior midfielders:

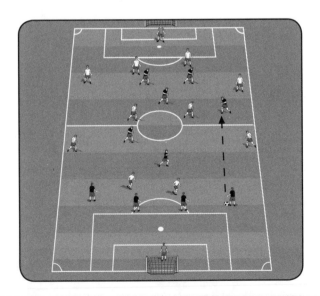

- or moving outwardly a forward.

We can also send a couple of midfielders inside to create difficulty for the opponent's defensive system.

This move keep our low playmaker free.

But, even without those movements it's hard for a 4-4-2 to play against two playmakers. SO, if the ball come to our low playmakers, he have many passing options:

-   to the midfielders

-   to the midfielders

- to the attacking midfielder;

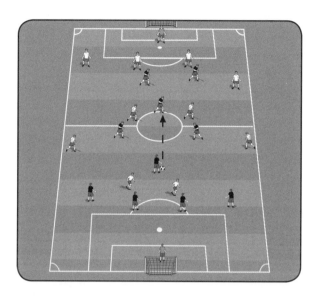

- to the wide defenders

With the ball to a forward open wide, they can utilize an outside overlap by a midfielder; a slant inside by the attacking midfielder and a run inside from the other central midfielder to create a number of options to challenge the 4-4-2.

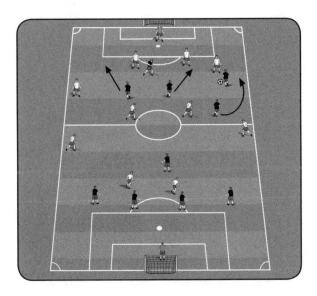

In the defensive phase, the Mourinho's 4-3-1-2 at Chelsea didn't leave the attacking midfielder (Ballack) just with offensive duties.

Otherwise, Ballack had to come back and collapse down with the rest of the team, building a wall of two lines of coverage and switching the 4-3-1-2 formation to a 4-4-2 patter.

If the attacking midfielder is on the opposite side of the ball when the ball is lost, he had to collapse back running on his zone

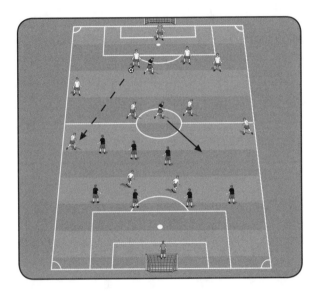

If the ball come to an opponent in a crossing area, the 3 holding midfielders have the goal to collapse down to protect the defensive group. In this way, we can see that the first overall goal of Mourinho is to keep the team compact and to have a numerical advantage in the defensive phase.

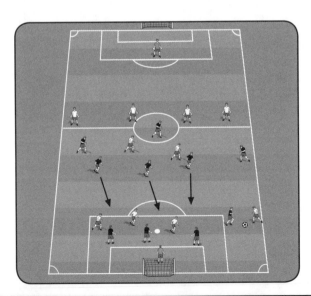

Sir Alex Ferguson's
4 - 4 - 2

Manchester United

Sir Alex Ferguson's 4-4-2 features are:
- the great utilization of the wings in the offensive phase
- the collective sense, where all the players are ready to help one another
- the goals scored in open play by combinations between the forwards
- huge utilization of crosses into the box
- quick counterattack, starting deep or at midfield position (long and medium counterattacks)
- close the opponent's spaces
- great utilization of set pieces
- balance between the offensive and the defensive phase

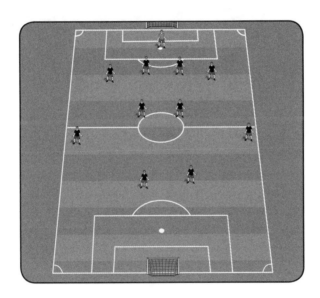

Ferguson often switched his formation from a 4-4-2 to a 4-2-3-1, a 4-4-1-1 in the defensive phase, using 2 holding midfielders and 2 wings behind 2 attackers: one of those attackers was a lone forward, the other was a second forward utilized as an attacking midfielder (Argentinean Carlos Tevez played this role). So we can add to the Ferguson's 4-4-2 pattern a common feature with the Mourinho's 4-3-3: flexibility. Ferguson isn't anchored to a lone pattern.

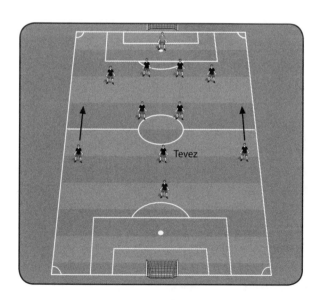

The 1999 midfielder was formed by Roy Keane and Paul Scholes in the middle, with Ryan Giggs, and David Beckham on the flanks.

That put players with different skills in the middle of the field, with a holding midfielder in Keane, a crosser in Beckham, a creativity player in Giggs and an holding midfielder able to run inside and score in Scholes.

Otherwise, Ferguson changed his tactical approach, having different players in his roster. With Christiano Ronaldo and Giggs on the flanks and two quick, technical players like Wayne Rooney and Carlos Tevez up top, he opted to play the ball on the ground and to line up two holding midfielders to guard his defensive four.

Obviously, the features of the 4-4-2 patterns used by Ferguson has been changed with the change of the players over the years.

We can find some differences between the classic 4-4-2 of Ferguson's first years in Manchester and latest edition of this formation.

In the early seasons, the fullbacks were ready to jump forward, not only to overlap the wingers, but to play a towing action. Meaning, to stay behind the wing to give him support.

Latest season, with two wings as Giggs and Christiano Ronaldo, who like to go inside between the line, there is more space for the backs to run forward and to provide support offensively.

By the way, as with Mourinho, Ferguson's first goal is to be able to cover defensively.

And, when Ferguson runs a 4-2-3-1 pattern, he lines up the formation with 2 blocks:
- one defensive block, including the four man back line and two holding midfielder like Michael Carrick and Darren Fletcher;

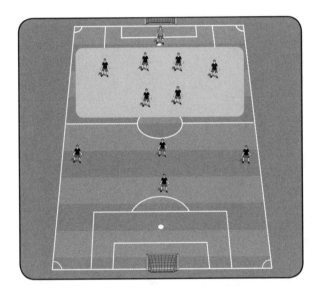

- one offensive block, including the four attacking players, 2 wingers and 2 forwards, one in front of the other.

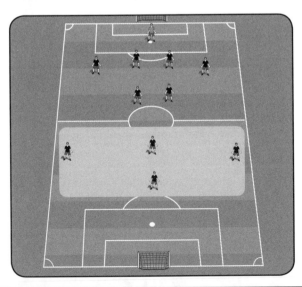

According to circumstances, Ferguson also played with a 4-3-3 pattern, with 3 central midfielder and 3 forwards.

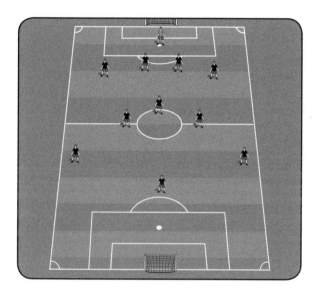

The one constant among all of his formations is a four man defense.

When it is possible, Ferguson's 4-4-2 attacks start from the defenders, especially from the centre-halves.

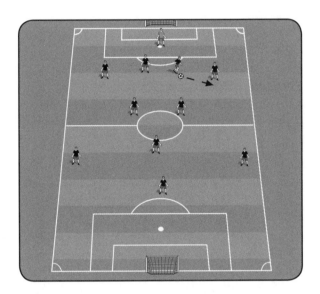

When this isn't possible, due to an high opponent's pressure, Manchester resorts to a long ball, often send towards a wide midfielder.

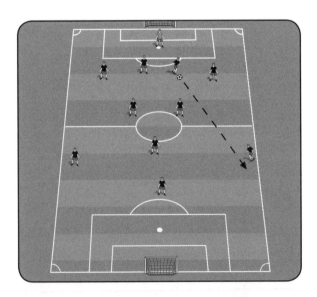

Those long balls can be sent by the keeper as well because both Peter Schmeichel and Edwin Van der Sar are able to make accurate long passes.

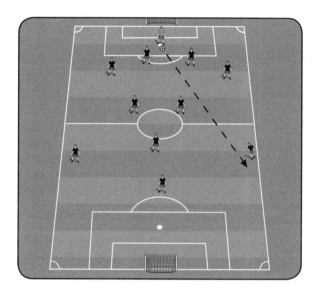

Another strength of Manchester United was the ability for Ferguson to switch the positions of his players, moving a player from the right wing to the attacking midfielder spot or from an attacking midfielder to a left wing position.

Here are some ways that the 4-4-2 could be adjusted to play against the 4-3-3.

How can a team take advantage of a 4-4-2 pattern against a 4-3-3 formation?

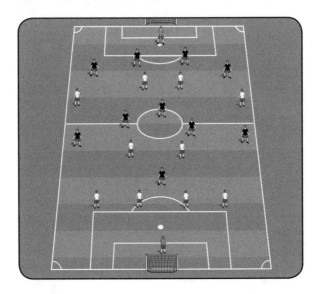

The 4-4-2 has an numerical advantage in defense, when 4-4-2 plays against a lone forward.

So, the offensive action can start from the defense.

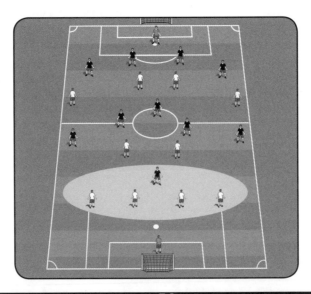

If, as often happens, the opponent's opt to play a high pressure in their attacking third by sending the wings up to support the lone forward in a pressing tactics, the 4-4-2 can will always play 4 v 3.

The 4-4-2 has a man free to play to

- The fullback can show for a through ball

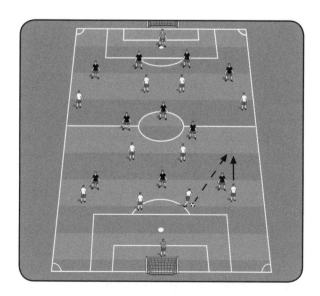

- playing a pass to the central midfielder (which will have an advantage against his central midfielder opponent (being closer to our defenders) to free the fullback for a run down the line.

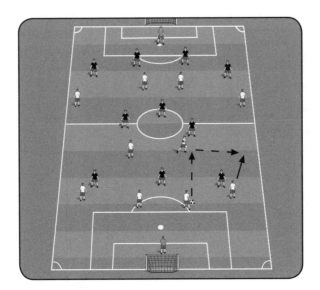

- sending the ball towards the wing who moves himself meet the ball in a space between the defensive and midfielder lines.

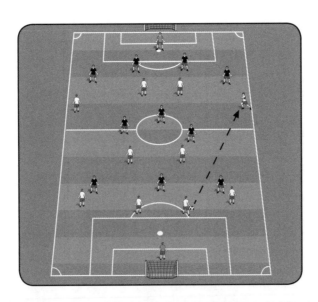

- changing the field with a pass to the opposite wing

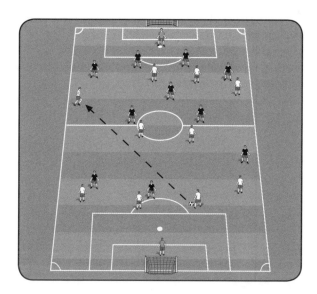

- finding the forward with a direct pass as he is moving toward the ball.

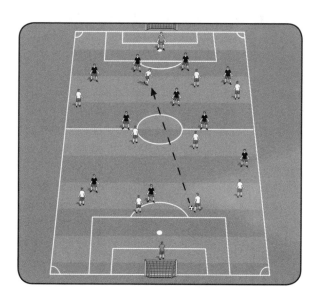

Each of these options give 4-4-2 a number of ways to create scoring chances against a 4-3-3 pattern.

With an overlapping movement by the full back, the 4-4-2 forces a central midfielder to go out to cover the fullback

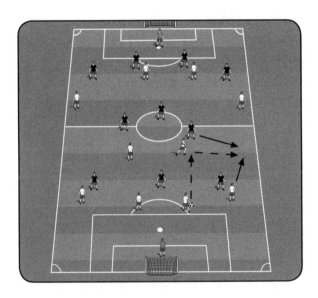

This is a very advanced position for the fullback. The defender in the 4-3-3 will stay back to cover the space.

This allows the fullback to pass the ball to:
- the central midfielder who has moved up
- the wing can go deep to keep the fullback busy
- one of the forwards which meet the ball

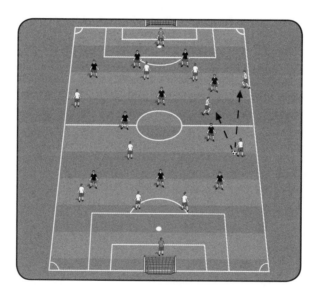

In this situation, it will be hard for the central back to move to cover the forward because he risks leaving too much space on behind him and to leaves the other central defender in a difficult 1-to-1 situation against the second forward.

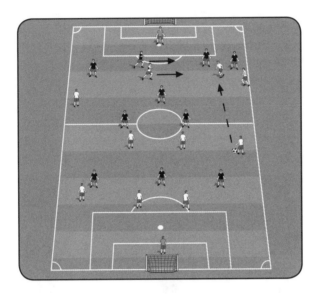

If the opponents opt to play a short diagonal, the fullback can switch the ball to the opposite wing.

If the opponents opt to collapse the holding midfielder in order to re-build the defensive line, a team playing a 4-4-2 can play with a 2v1 advantage in the middle.

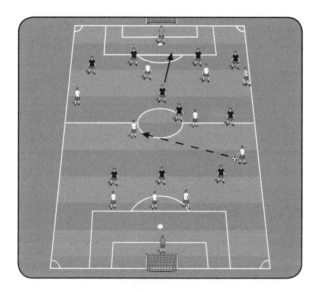

Another option is to play the ball back for the midfielder to pass to the overlapping fullback. This creates a 2 v 1 situation on the outside: wing and fullback against the fullback.

If a central midfielder collapses down to play against our wing, the wing can send the ball:
- to a central midfielder creating a 2 v 2 situation;
- send the ball back to the fullback who can move the ball to the forwards

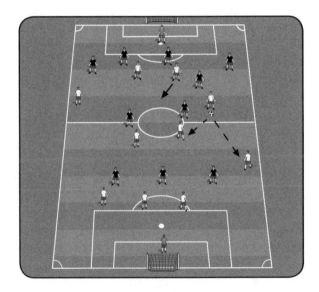

If the opponent's wings are able to collapse back to cover in the defensive phase, they won't be able to do it for the whole match, if they are true offensive wings. They just won't have the energy to cover the space.

If they are able to do it for the whole match, they probably loose the ability to be creative in attack.

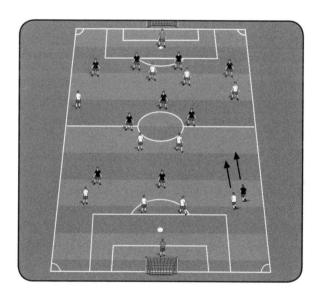

With a ball directly towards a central forwards, 4-4-2 have some options:
  - ball back to a midfielder then a pass towards a slanting run by the other
    forwards

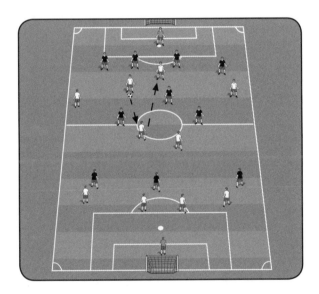

Ball back from the forward to a central midfielder and then played towards a winger on his side to play a 1 v 1 situation.

Ball from the central midfielder towards the opposite wing to play another 1 v 1 situation.

Obviously, those are option if the opponents, as often happens, move the central defender to cover the forward. If that doesn't happen, the forward can turn and go towards the goal.

Or pass to the other forward making a slanted run.

How to use the 4-4-2 against a 4-3-1-2

If the opponents runs a 4-3-1-2 pattern, the 4-4-2 has to attack utilizing the numerical superiority on the flanks, where the 4-4-2 can play a 2 v 1.

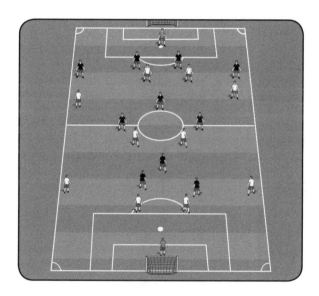

The first option, from the defense, will be to move the ball outside.

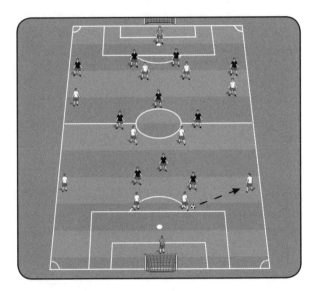

This pass will force the opponents' to slide a midfielder laterally, freeing space in the middle. So the fullback can send the ball to the wing for a 1v1 or to the central midfielder, who can play a 2 v 2 situations in the middle.

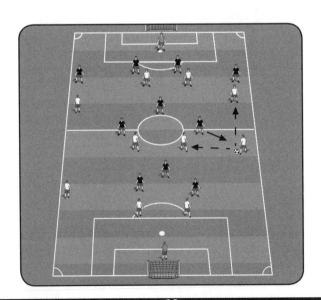

To create a numerically superiority, we can bring a forward back to the ball.

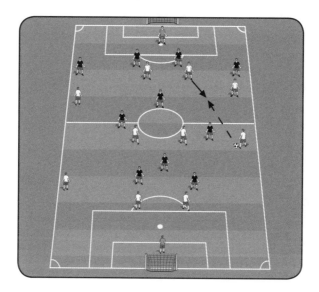

What will the opponents do? If the central back mark the forward, we will have a dangerous 3 v 3 situation in their defense.

If the opponent's cover the forward with the holding midfielder, or send the holding midfielder into the defensive line, we will have a dangerous space to exploit between the lines.

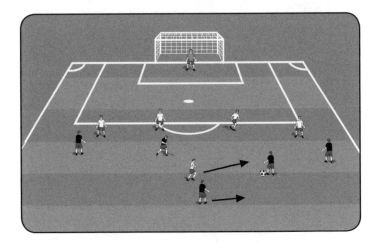

If the opponents collapse the attacking midfielder, we can:
- a change of field;

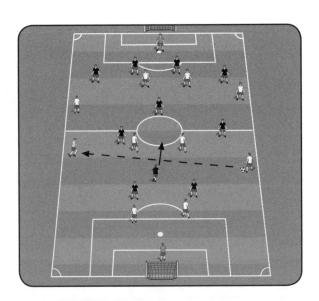

- or a ball to the winger who can play a combination with the forward

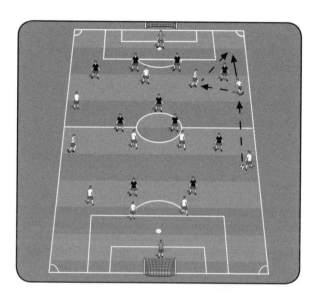

In the 2007/08 season, Manchester United won the European Champions League.

The starting line up in the Final against Chelsea, formerly Josè Mourinho's team, was a 4-4-1-1, with a four man back line, two men as holding midfielders in Michael Carrick and Paul Schole; Owen Hargreaves and Christiano Ronaldo on the flanks; Carlos Teves up top just behind Wayne Rooney.

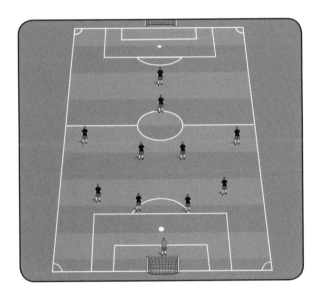

Alex Ferguson put his team ahead with three moves:
- employing Christiano Ronaldo on the left
- utilizing Hargreaves as defensive wing
- utilizing a corner kick to take the lead

Having Hargreaves as right wing gave Ferguson the opportunity to close the link between Chelsea's dangerous attacking left back Ashley Cole and the attacking players.

Also, Hargreaves had the defensive knowledge to get back when the team were defending.

A 1-2 punch leaves Wes Brown free to sends a cross into the box which finds Christiano Ronaldo, a strong header, in a 1-to-1 situation against the Chelsea's defense. Ronaldo easily scored.

After the goal, Manchester United takes control of the tempo utilizing its ability to keep possession and defending with a 4-5 player wall when the ball was lost. They played fast counterattacks after the ball is won.

Having two men up top, gives Ferguson the chance to pressure the central-havles very high up the pitch.

Also, closing the centre, Manchester United make hard for Chelsea to play through Claude Makelele.

In the second half, when Chelsea gained momentum, Alex Ferguson stayed conservative, showing his great ability to read the game.

With the Blues pressuring over and over again, he switched his 4-4-1-1 pattern into a more pure 4-5-1 formation.

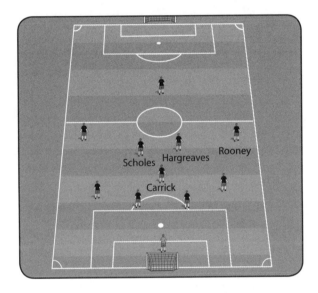

To do it, Ferguson moved Wayne Rooney on the right flank, pairing Hargreaves in the middle with Carrick and Scholes.

It's clear that with a 4-3-3/4-5-1 formation Manchester united has more points from which to attack, especially from counterattacks.

Many fans think of the 4-5-1 as a negative formation because it could mean a negative attitude and a negative approach, a defensive approach, to the matches.

Alex Ferguson showed that this is not necessarily true.

Ferguson tried to adapt his patter to the opponents, playing a 4-4-2 or a 4-4-1-1 in the English Premier League and playing a more 'European' style patter as 4-3-3/4-5-1 in Europe.

With the 4-5-1 pattern, Ferguson displays a more pragmatic formation, able to contain but also able to run his much loved counterattacks.

With the 4-5-1, and with the wings able to come back in the defensive phase, Ferguson has the chance have an extra midfielder on the field, especially on the away from home.

This extra man in the middle gives the them the opportunity to better cover the defensive back line and also to have more areas to escape from the opponent's pressure and to run counterattacks.

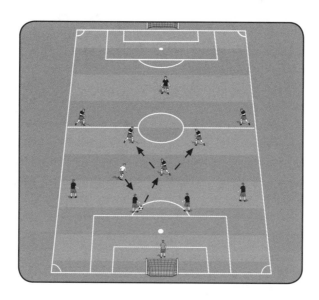

In the 08/09 season, Manchester United brought in Bulgarian striker Dymitar Berbatov.

With the former Tottenham forward, Ferguson has another option up top. Against Danish side of Aalborg, Ferguson lined up a 4-4-2 pattern with Christiano Ronaldo and Nani as wingers and Berbatov paired with Wayne Rooney as forwards.

The three goals scored against Aalborg are a clear example of the utilization of Berbatov in the Manchester starting line-up.

The third goal scored by Berbatov came after a great counterattack action. Manchester's midfielder threaded the ball to Carlos Tevez on the middle.

Tevez slipped a pass to the right for Christiano Ronaldo who beat the defender and crossed into the middle where Berbatov, coming from behind, and Tevez had a cross action to cover the first-post and the central-box zone.

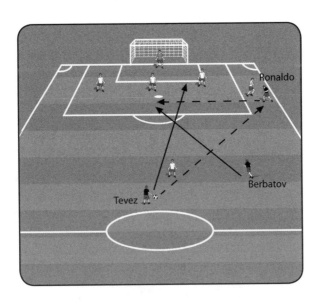

The 1-0 lead came from an inside pass from the middle by Ryan Giggs to Wayne Rooney.

The action started with a slant move of Nani on the right. You can see as Manchester cover all the offensive field with all its four offensive players: 2 spread wings and 2 central forwards.

Other goals from this season showed that Alex Ferguson continues to stress the concept of spreading the offense out, opening the opponent's defensive system in order to create two offensive option for his team:
- first is to attack down the middle with his two forwards,
- second is to open the field externally in order to cross the ball into the box.

A great offensive weapon for Ferguson's Manchester United is the ability to attack the spaces with counterattacking plays.

Ferguson likes to send a lot of players forward on counterattacks.

Having a lot of players up top causes many problems for an unbalanced team.

Against Liverpool, in a counterattack action, a long ball came to Berbatov, who slipped a reverse pass into the middle.

With two players covering an attacking teammate, Teves was completely free to run into the middle and score alone in the box coming from a deep position.

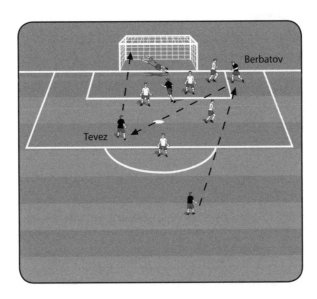

The 08/09 edition of Manchester United, just like the previous season's version have much more to them than just Christiano Ronaldo.

The work of Scholes and Hargreaves is very important: they have to find a balance between the offensive, the defensive and the transition between the two phases.

Berbatov also in the mix and with the development of Nani, Alex Ferguson can continue to mix his offensive threats.

This mix happens not only before they take the field but during the match, with the wings and the forwards able to exchange their field position in order to confuse the opponents.

In the defensive phase, Manchester United has some trouble because the defense isn't always solid.

The squad try to solve the defensive issues with a collective effort: every player runs and helps the team in the defensive phase.

Offensively, when the ball is won, the first option is to organize a very quick counterattack.

We had an example in the match United won against West Bromwich Albion.

The first goal came after a long pass from behind which put Wayne Rooney in a 1 v 1 situation against a WBA's defender

Rooney was the target again for the pass which created the fourth goal.

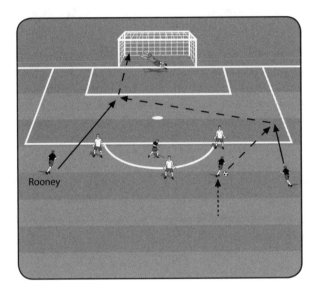

With the opponent unbalanced, Manchester United was able to send as many players as possible to the opponent's half of the pitch, switching from a defensive to an offensive action.

Lightning counter-attacks and players that are very good in 1 v 1 situations are deliberate tactic.

Mourinho's Key Chelsea Players

The Key Players in Josè Mourinho's Chelsea Teams

Petr Cech

He's one of the best goalkeeper in the world. Tactically, to have a strong keeper in the back is a very, very important key to a good defense. A good netminder not only prevents the opponents from scoring but also give the defense confidence.

He is also a good passer, so he can play long ball to start quickly counter-attacks.

John Terry

The England national team standout is an amazing defender. He's a real defensive skipper. He's the leader of the four man back line of Josè Mourinho patterns, both in a 4-3-1-2 formation or a 4-4-2.

He has the size and the height to be effective in the Premiership, which is suited to big men.

Despite his size, he has good speed. He is also very dangerous when he moves up for corner kicks.

Ashley Cole

This fullback is an important key to Mourinho's patterns. He has speed, quickness, agility and good technical skills.

Having a fullback with this characteristics is very important for a team because:
-   he cover all the outside;
-   he provides good crosses into the opponent's box
-   he provides good passes to attacking players

Defensively, his speed is used to recover against the opponent's counterattack and to play quick diagonals, supporting the central backs.

Claude Makelele

He was the holding midfielder of the Mourinho's era at Chelsea.

Makekele is a typical holding midfielder. He doesn't have great technical skills but he plays with intensity, contentiousness and application.

His play is a smart, quick, physical player. He provided a screen in front of Mourinho's four man defensive back line, in both the 4-3-3 or 4-3-1-2 formations.

Having a players like Makelele is a tremendous advantage for a team. In fact, with this type of player on the roster, a coach can play a bit more offensively, moving the fullbacks up and playing with one or two attacking midfielders. Also, this player intercepted a large number of balls, breaking the opponent's attack and starting a lot of dangerous and quick counterattack for his team.

Geremi
This is a player often underestimated but really important to the balance of Mourinho's squads.

He's a perfect complement for his Makelele, providing a lot of smart play in the offensive and defensive phases.

Defensively, having a player as big and strong as Geremi on a roster means you have a 'ball hunter' you can pair him with another midfielder with similar skills (as Mourinho did with Makelele), create a formidable wall in front of the defense.

Also, his speed and strength give the team a lot of power on the offensive side of the ball, especially in counterattacking situations.

Frank Lampard
See earlier in the book. (Page 27)

Arjen Robbe, Damine Duff, Shwan Wright-Phillips, Joe Cole: these players add quality, speed, quickness, 1 v 1 ability, crosses, good passes and set pieces. To sum it up, they are all great offensive weapons. Their runs on the field are the key to quick counterattacks. Their physical ability gives the team a chance to destroy the opponents' counter attacks collapsing quickly to support the defensive backline.

Didier Drogba
This player is the key of the whole system. He scores, and a forward has to score first. But Drogba didn't have to do this work alone in Mourinho's formations. He played as a pivot player, giving the team the opportunity to move up and play quick counterattacks.

His presence forced opponents to play with a very deep defense, keeping the squad long.

Ferguson's Key Manchester Utd Players

The Key Players in Sir Alex Ferguson's Manchester United

Edwin Van der Sar

This player isn't a great keeper but is a good player tactically. His long passes are the key to start quick counterattacks and to give defenders a safety valve against the opponent's pressure.

Having a keeper with this playing skills is important because he gives team another defender.

Jaap Stam

This former Ferguson's defender was one of the strongest defenders in the modern era.

He had size, he was tall and strong, he was a good header of the ball both defensively and offensively.

He didn't have quickness but, despite his size, he had speed so he was able to play in a very high defense position due to his ability recovery.

He was also strong in 1 v 1 situations, he was a tactical force.

Having a player with his skills is important, because he can play in the trenches if the opponents press or move up the field, as discussed earlier.

Roy Keane, Paul Ince

They are all typical holding midfielders.

Having one or two players like Keane and Ince allowed for the presence of many offensive players in Ferguson's teams.

They give team balance and force in the middle, building a wall in front of the defense.

Ryan Giggs, Christiano Ronaldo

These players give the team creativity and 1 v 1 ability. Their ability to dribble creates many numerical superiority situations. Their speed also give team the opportunity to play quick counterattack.

David Beckham

He is a different type of winger. Better suited as central midfielder by many coaches. Beckham's skills give the team a lot of scoring options.

He can score directly with set pieces or create scoring chances by crossing the ball from the outside.

His long ball gives team the chance to play a fast tempo on counterattacks. His ability on corner kicks created a lot of goalscoring opportunities.

He also played both ends of the field, making a contribution on defense as well.

Dwight Yorke, Carlos Tevez, Wayne Rooney

These are three different types of attackers who have some skills in common: they are small, speedy players.

Their technical skills give the team the ability to possess the ball on the ground.

Their speed creates a chance to counter attacks while their quickness permit them to easily beat the opponents' defenders into the box.

Also, they are smart players, able to find the spaces and to play against any defensive system.

What We Can Learn From Mourinho and Ferguson

Obviously, there are many things we can learn from these coaches and many things they have in common.

Starting with the tactical aspects, we can see that they stress the utilization of a four men back line. This choice gives the coaches the opportunity to cover the whole defensive front.

Also, teaching a four man back line is simpler than teaching a team to player with a three men back line.

The four men defensive back line is a defense that is better known by the players, English and Latin alike (Mourinho trained in Portugal).

Ferguson utilizes more attacking fullbacks, sending the outside defenders forward, while Mourinho likes to have defenders focused on their defensive duties.

By the way, both coaches like to play with central defenders able to pass. This provides another safety valve to the midfielder if the opponents press.

In front of the defensive front, both coaches like to have a couple of holding midfielders.

Those midfielders are a key to obtaining balance, which is one of the most important things they look for in their team's play.

When Ferguson had a uncommon wingers like Beckham, he used a lone holding midfielder such as Roy Keane.

But this player was able to cover the whole field horizontally, and the presence of Beckham allows another man to follow the opponent's in Manchester's defensive zone.

Ferguson lines up a central attacking midfielder in Paul Scholes, who gives him a player able to contain the opponents and able to find the opponent's net.

The role played by Paul Scholes was played by Frank Lampard in Mourinho's Chelsea team.

Lampard is more of a technical player then Scholes. He can deliver some nice touches and passes as well, but the penetrating skills are the similar.

By the way, both midfields have some strong player, able to score from distance.

Things change up top.

Ferguson lined up players able to change their position in the course of the match, confusing the opponent's defensive systems. They are able to play in multiple spots.

Otherwise, Mourinho likes to have pure wingers. This way, he gets more crosses into the middle and more players able to collapse down to help the midfield in defensive transition situations.

Up top, Mourinho likes to line up a lone forward, strong, tall and able to hold the ball and allow the team to push up.

However, Ferguson often lined up two forwards, paired in the same line or with one high and one low.

In this way, he has two offensive options up front, while defensively he brings back an attacker to press the opponent's playmaker and to be ready as a first weapon in the counterattacks.

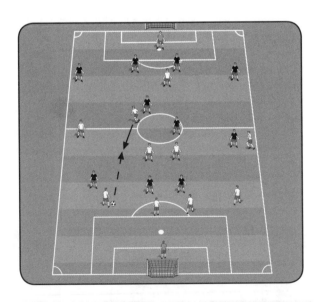

About the high defense, there is a big difference between Mourinho's Chelsea and Porto.

In fact, at Porto Mourinho utilized 4-3-3 and 4-3-1-2 patterns, but with some tactical differences.

Mourinho's Porto was more suited to possessing the ball, and played with more short passes.

He also pressed higher and more frequently.

So, while Chelsea was a counterattacking team, Porto was a more traditional Latin team: organized and technical.

Both coaches stress the team's compactness: every player has to help the others, running on the field.

Both coaches like flexibility: they are not anchored to a lone system or to a lone tactical playbook.

As Mourinho moved from Porto to Chelsea, Ferguson too changed his playing style over the years at Manchester.

He switched from a team suited to crossing from the outside into the box to a team mate who is utilized more for central attacks.

First Ferguson's Manchester additions.

Lastly, Ferguson's Manchester editions.

At the end, psychologically, both coaches stress hard work, and both trust in their players.

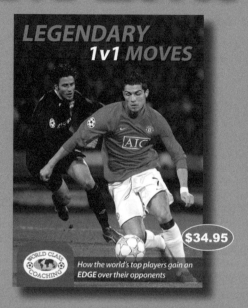

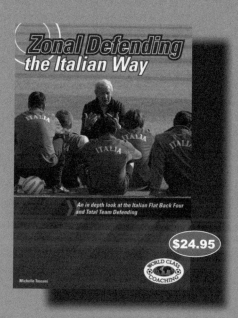